MW01074191

A TALE OF
DEATH
AND
GLORY

The Acts of Saint Sebastian
and His Companions

SAINT AMBROSE OF MILAN

TRANSLATED BY

FR. ROBERT NIXON, OSB

TAN Books
Gastonia, North Carolina

Translated by Fr. Robert Nixon, OSB

Cover design by Andrew Schmalen
Cover image: St. Sebastian by Perugino, c. 290, photographed by Ann Ronan Pictures/ Print Colllector/ Getty Images.

ISBN: 978-1-5051-2826-0
Kindle ISBN: 978-1-5051-2827-7
ePUB ISBN: 978-1-5051-2828-4

Published in the United States by
TAN Books
PO Box 269
Gastonia, NC 28053
www.TANBooks.com

A TALE OF
DEATH
AND
GLORY

Contents

⟫⟫ ─── Translator's Note ⟶

AMONG THE VAST, glorious, and almost innumerable company of martyrs of the early Church, Saint Sebastian stands out as one of the most widely revered and venerated. Saint Sebastian lived during the time of Emperor Diocletian in the late third century. He was a high-ranking soldier distinguished by his intelligence, courage, and talent. He performed his duties as a soldier in meritorious and exemplary fashion while working vigorously and inconspicuously to support other Christians, especially those who faced persecution and hardships. The legendary story of his cruel transfixion by a multitude of arrows is one of the most popular themes of Western religious iconography and has been depicted by artists including Botticelli, Titian, and El Greco.

The written accounts of the deeds, sufferings, and death of the martyrs may be considered one of the very earliest genres of Christian literature. In both Latin and Greek (as well as Coptic and Syriac), countless histories of early martyrs appeared. These histories range from brief and rudimentary outlines of events to polished and refined artistic productions. Amongst the latter category, the *Acta Sancti Sebastiani*, presented here in an English translation for the first time, must be accorded primacy of place. It is a complex and sophisticated work, encompassing a great many characters and events, almost in the manner of a modern adventure novel.

The *Acta Sancti Sebastiani* is traditionally attributed to Saint Ambrose of Milan (c. 339–97), the great fourth-century Doctor of the Church, who was renowned as an outstanding homilist, exegete, and hymnographer. The date of the work and the style of the writing are all consistent with this attribution, and Saint Sebastian (as a native of Milan) would have been particularly important to Saint Ambrose and his congregation.

The story of Saint Sebastian and his companions is a work of considerable sophistication and serves not only to relate and record actions of heroic sanctity but also to convey a message of fidelity and courage and to expound with radiant clarity the doctrines and theology of the Church. Indeed, in the long discourses of Saint Sebastian and other characters in the story, one can often perceive something of the eloquent and learned voice of the author, Saint Ambrose, shining through.

The form of Christianity portrayed in the work is a distinctly "Roman" one, exemplifying the virtues of manly courage, self-sacrifice, loyalty, and honesty. In the various powerful arguments for the truth of the faith which are articulated, the doctrine is entirely and purely Christian, but the values extolled by Stoic philosophy—endurance, patience, detachment from passing things, and acceptance of that which is inevitable—can also be quite clearly perceived.

Today, those who are loyal to the Catholic faith face many serious adversities, both overt and covert, from governments and authorities. The latter often strive to impose values which are contrary to Christ and His Church's teachings just as in the times of Diocletian and Maximian.

In this context, the story of Saint Sebastian and his companions, which is a true "tale of blood and glory," presents an inspiring example of those qualities of fidelity and courage which continue to be so urgently necessary for all Catholics today.

Sancte Sebastiane, ora pro nobis!

Fr. Robert Nixon, OSB
Abbey of the Most Holy Trinity
New Norcia, Western Australia

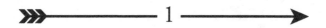

1

Sebastian, a devout and sincere Christian, was born in our own beautiful city of Milan. He also enjoyed citizenship of the city of Narbonne through patrilineal descent. At the time when he lived, Diocletian and Maximian held power as co-emperors,[1] and Sebastian was greatly honored and esteemed by both of them. He was a most distinguished soldier and a man of outstanding wisdom and talent, and so he had been appointed to the illustrious rank of commander of the first cohort[2] of the imperial army. The two emperors, though themselves both godless and impious men, greatly valued and appreciated his constant presence at their court.

---

[1] Diocletian ruled as emperor from 284 to 305. During most of that time, he shared power with a co-emperor, Maximian.

[2] The rank of commander of the first cohort was considered to be one of the most powerful positions in the Roman army, commanding eight hundred elite soldiers, or five centurions. The first cohort was also the most critical cohort in battle, for they led the initial attack.

Sebastian was ever-ready with prudent and intelligent advice. He was honest and candid, energetic, reliable, competent, and in all respects a thoroughly honorable man. His soldiers loved him as if he were a father to them, and all who were at the palace venerated him with profound and sincere regard. For Sebastian was a worshipper of the true God, and each person who is filled with the gifts of Divine grace and who cultivates real virtue will always tend to be well-esteemed by his fellows in every place and time.

Sebastian diligently offered daily prayers to Christ with all humility and reverence. Yet he did this secretly and kept his faith hidden from the eyes of the emperors. For Diocletian and Maximian were both fanatical persecutors of the Christian religion. But the reason Sebastian concealed his faith from them was not that he was afraid of death or torture, nor that he was reluctant to lose his high position and the wealth and prestige which accompanied it. Rather, he knew that by serving well at the court and exercising a role of leadership in the army, he would be able to encourage and assist his many fellow Christians who faced persecutions and hardships and embolden them to be steadfast in their faith—to the bitter end if necessary. Indeed, Sebastian's words of encouragement and exhortation had fortified the minds of many to face the bloody terrors of martyrdom without flinching, and thus to attain the golden crown of eternal glory.

Among those whom he encouraged were two twin brothers, Marcus and Marcellianus, men of illustrious lineage and considerable wealth. These two brothers had both been imprisoned on account of their allegiance to the Christian faith, and they were arrested and held in chains. But every day, Sebastian would go to visit them and pray with them, offering them all the spiritual support he possibly could.

Both Marcus and Marcellianus, as well as their servants who had been incarcerated with them, were subjected to a variety of cruel tortures in an effort to induce them to renounce their faith in Christ. Yet thanks to Sebastian's encouragement, they remained steadfast and unwavering. For they saw that all earthly things were passing and that whatever torments they now suffered would seem to be but a momentary dream in comparison with the everlasting and infinite bliss of heaven. Thus fortified by the potent medicine of faith, all traces of fear were dispelled from the hearts of these two courageous and holy brothers.

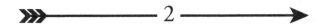

2

So THE TWINS Marcus and Marcellianus were blessed and strengthened with every spiritual consolation while they were held in captivity. They faced all the torments of their torturers with patient endurance and courage. Since they adamantly refused to renounce their faith, the fatal sentence of beheading was passed upon them. But they were told that if they should agree to sacrifice to the pagan idols of Rome, their lives would be spared and they would be returned to their parents, wives, and children unharmed and have all their property and status restored to them.

Now, as we have noted, these men were both affluent and of high standing. Their father was a prominent citizen by the name of Tranquillinus, and their mother was a good but simple woman called Marcia. They came to visit their twin sons in prison, and they were accompanied by the wives and children of both Marcus and Marcellianus.

Being an influential and well-respected family, Tranquillinus and Marcia had prevailed upon the authorities to grant their sons a generous period of time before they faced execution. So they were given some thirty days before the sentence of death was to be carried out. And if Marcus and Marcellianus should consent to burn incense before the pagan idols during this time of respite, they were assured that they would be granted their lives and their freedom.

Moved by the bonds of natural and familial affection, their parents (who were not Christians) naturally tried to convince them to renounce their faith and thus to escape death. "How is it that you have such stubborn minds and such unfeeling hearts," their father said, "that you bring this anxiety to me, your gray-haired father, and that you so cruelly renew the birth pangs of your dear mother who brought you forth into this world? For when she gave birth to you, the pains which she felt then were assuaged by the joy of bringing a child into the world—and not one child only but twin sons! I also, as your father, felt a double affection of paternity for you both. But now you bring to us, your father and mother, inconsolable pains. You inflict on us wounds which can never heal by your stubbornness. For by your deaths all our hopes and joys shall be taken away from us! Our family's reputation shall be irreparably besmirched and our honor shall be utterly destroyed. We shall be disgraced as well as heartbroken. Do you not feel any pity or compassion?

"Oh, what madness is it that makes you seem to desire the grim horror of death more than fearing it? I beg you, my twin beloved sons, cease this nonsense and do whatever you must do to save your lives, for in saving your lives, you shall save also our happiness and peace. And remember that you yourselves are both fathers of your own wonderful children! Would you abandon them too and leave them wretched and fatherless to face this cruel and cold world alone and unguarded?"

Tranquillinus continued reproaching his sons in this manner for some time. Then Marcia, the mother of Marcus and Marcellianus, now approached them. She was in a state of abject despair and agitation, her gray hair disarrayed and her countenance trembling with febrile emotion. She then showed her tearful, wrinkled face and hands to her sons[3] and exclaimed, "My precious children, behold the elderly mother who once nursed you and who suckled you when you were helpless infants! You both are dearer to me than life itself. In your faces I see the likeness of your father, my beloved husband, and also something of my own image. Throughout all your lives, you have both been diligent and loving sons, and you are both all that your father and myself could ever hope for!

"But now I am surrounded by bitter sorrow from every side! Unstoppable tears well up in my eyes, for I shall be deprived not of one child only but of both my sons in this one horrendous thing. Surely, there is no grief which can be compared to mine! I shall lose both my sons at once. If you had been killed in war by an enemy, you should know that I would take a sword in my own aged hand and go out and wreak furious revenge on your killers. If you had been falsely accused and unjustly cast into

---

[3] The Latin text at this point reads: *"Et cunctis fletentibus ostendat eis laxis pellibus quas suxerant mammas."*

prison, I myself would have willingly joined you in your dungeon and happily perished with you. But this is a new form of dying, a new species of madness, which possesses you! For you both could easily escape death simply by honoring the old gods. But instead you seem to invite your executioner to come and carry out his sentence by your sheer and headstrong obstinacy. And—just as this new madness deludes you—so a new and unprecedented form of grief comes over me and breaks my heart to a thousand pieces. For you who are young embrace death of your own volition, while I who am old am compelled to go on living in the bitterness of despair!"

While their mother continued to bewail her fate and the stubbornness (as she saw it) of her sons, their father bent over and took up a handful of dust from the ground. This he threw over his gray head, and he raised his voice to heaven in a desperate cry, speaking thus, "I have come here to bid a final farewell to my sons, who wish to depart from me and to die! Alas, the tomb which I have prepared for myself in my old age I shall now use to bury my sons, who are still in their youth!

"O my sons, you should be the staff that supports me in my old age and the two lights which illuminate the darkness of my decrepitude. You were born happily and formed as fine citizens! Your mother and I gave you every opportunity in life. You have been blessed with intelligence and the best possible education that can be had. What is this insanity that now makes you long for death? For death should never please those who are truly alive and animated with healthy vitality. It is not a friend to be courted. Rather, all people of sound mind shun it and flee from it, and accept it only when it is unavoidable.

"Of course, in the end we all must die. But the fact that death is something inevitable does not make it something which we should hasten to embrace. You are both filled with exuberant health, talents, and all good gifts. Why seek death when there is so much for you to enjoy in life?

"O come to me, old men, and weep with me over my sons who will leave me alone and unsupported in my old age! O come to me, all you who are still young, and weep over these foolish offspring of mine who would throw away the blessings of youth! Let my eyes be blinded over with tears, so I shall see no more of this madness! Let me not behold the beloved sons of my own flesh and blood fall to the edge of the sword. For they are so dear to me that if a mere stick should touch them I should tremble with grief and fear, and if I should see them hurt in any way, my own heart would break with infinite sorrow!"

As the old man said these words and other things of a similar nature, the wives of both Marcus and Marcellianus drew near to them, together with their small children and infant offspring. Overcome with emotion, they displayed the babies they bore in their arms to their husbands. With voices almost choked with sadness and anxiety, they cried out, "To whose embrace are you so callously leaving us? Why are you so recklessly abandoning the bonds of married love? For if you depart from us, who shall be the master of our household and the father to these children? What is this beastly and wicked cruelty that makes you turn your back on those you love, to cast off your parents, to reject your wives, and to abandon your children? What is it that makes you forget those whom you love and who love you and instead to seek so avidly the cold and hateful hand of the executioner?"

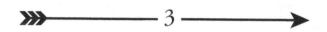

3

MARCUS AND MARCELLIANUS listened to the words of their mother, father, and wives with compassion and pity. As they heard their heartfelt reproaches and beheld their tears and sighs, as well as those of their young children, their own hearts were deeply touched. Their souls began to waver from their formerly firm resolution.

Now, Sebastian—as a commander of the imperial cohort—was also present at the time, waiting quietly in the background and witnessing and listening to all that transpired. Although he was in attendance as a court official and representative of the emperor, his real loyalty lay to the God of heaven and the Christian faith. The military garb which he wore of a soldier of Rome was a disguise for one who was more truly a soldier of Christ. And he realized that Marcus and Marcellianus, the two strong athletes of Jesus, were beginning to be fatigued under the strain of their struggle and that their resolve was starting to falter.

So he stood up in the midst of them all and raised his voice boldly: "O brave warriors of Christ, until now you have shown yourself to be skillful gladiators in the Divine battle! You have both drawn near the palm of glorious victory through your strength of heart and unwavering determination. Now are you, who have already overcome the torments of the torturer, going to be so easily overcome by mere tears and words? Shall you throw away an everlasting crown of glory for this?

"Stand firm and arm yourselves, not with weapons of steel, but with the invincible sword of faith! Do not permit your victory to be stolen away by the tears and sighs of women. You have already almost conquered the enemy of your salvation, the devil, and stand with your feet planted upon his cowering neck. Do not let him arise again and beat you! Raise yourselves up from all earthly affections; do not loosen your grasp now on the glorious trophy of immortal life which you hold in your hands for the sake of mere mortal tears and the crying of infants.

"For truly, these whom you see mourning and weeping now would rejoice if they were able to know the sacred and magnificent truth of what it is that you believe. They think that this earthly life is all there is, and that once we die there is no hereafter—that the soul vanishes when the body perishes. If they knew, as you know, that there is another life which follows physical death and that this life which follows is everlasting, free from all sorrow and filled with eternal and infinite bliss, then surely they would hasten with you to approach that glorious, eternal life! For compared to it, this passing existence here on earth would seem to be nothing but the play of insubstantial shadows.

"Indeed, this earthly life passes quickly, like a fleeting dream. It is so inconstant that even those who love it most dearly are not able to retain it for very long. It is truly an unfaithful mistress! From the very beginning of the world, this fleeting life has consistently betrayed all those who place their hopes in it and deceived all those who believe its vain and empty promises. Nothing here is certain; everything is in flux and illusory.

"But deceitfulness and inconstancy is not the only crime of which this mortal life is guilty. For she serves us up also the vices of gluttony and drunkenness, she brings the shipwreck of disaster upon helpless youths, and she infects the human heart with perverse and vain desires. Theft, conflict, and scandal are her constant companions. And it is love of this present life which is at the root of all crimes and works of evil. When a man kills his own brother, when a son kills his father, when a person is murdered by their own trusted friend, what is the wicked motivation or underlying desire or vile hope that leads to these nefarious deeds? If one investigates deeply enough, one will find that it is always love of the present life which is the root cause. For whenever people love life more than they love justice, then crime inevitably follows.

"Why do pirates sail the sea robbing other vessels by violence? Why do bandits waylay travelers? Why does the rich man oppress and exploit the poor? Why do the proud dominate the humble? Why does the wicked take advantage of the innocent? There is no other reason than love of this fleshly life and the desire to attain the vain and transitory things which pertain to it!

"It is thus love of this earthly existence which gives rise to all crimes, which prompts people to injustice, and which encourages them to sin. And what is the final reward that it gives to all those who love and serve her so ardently and eagerly? It is only this: everlasting death, a state of decay and dissolution from which there is no escape and no return. For out of the womb of this passing, mortal life, death is brought forth as a child. And so it happens that human beings, who were created to enjoy eternal life with God in heaven, become ensnared in this earthly valley of death! In the end, they go to the grave—or rather, to the ghastly and infernal nether-regions of hell!—carrying nothing with them but their burden of sin and shame.

"My friends, it is this same mortal life—which is inconstant, deceptive, and in the end, fatal—which would now seize upon your hearts and draw you away from the true life of eternal glory which awaits you!"

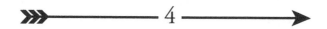

4

THEN SEBASTIAN TURNED his gaze to Tranquillinus and Marcia, the parents of the twin brothers. He addressed them, saying, "You are most assuredly both very good parents. But it behooves you to realize that your sons are now making their way to the court of heaven, to the realm of incorruptible honor, to the friendship and favor of the eternal Emperor! And yet you would hold them back from their glorious departure from this passing world by your misguided lamentations and bitter reproaches."

Turning to their wives, he continued, "And you, O most chaste and devoted wives, under the guise of piety and love, you are seeking to infect the heart of your dear husbands with impiety and unmanly cowardice. For it is not true death which they now approach but supreme liberty! For even if they did listen to you, it would mean only that they had the brief time of this mortal life to remain with you. And then you would be eternally separated by death anyway. And if you ever met again, it would only be among the dire and everlasting torments of the netherworld. There, the hungry flames forever devour the souls of the unbelievers. There, fearsome dragons unceasingly gnaw at the lips of those who have uttered blasphemy. There, venomous serpents viciously strike at the heart of those who have refused to believe in the one true God!

"Yes, there the moans and lamentations of lost souls ring out without respite, as they endure the constant scalding of the unquenchable fire and the unremitting torments of hell's fiendish torturers. There, there is no end to tribulation, and the sufferings in that place of terrors have neither conclusion nor termination, nor finish nor close. Always is that fire rekindled, and whatever has been incinerated grows once more only to be burnt away again and again, forever and ever."

Speaking to them all, he implored, "Oh, let your sons and your husbands escape from these fearful punishments and from this grim and deplorable fate! Permit them instead to ascend to the unfading crowns of victory for which they are destined by God. And do not fear! For they shall not be separated from you for long but shall be going before you to prepare for you your own star-illumined mansions in the limitless plains of heaven. In these celestial dwellings, you—together with your dear sons and beloved husbands—shall rejoice for all eternity.

"If, in this world, you are delighted with your houses fashioned from mere earthly stone, how much more should you be urged on to seek the beauty of those astral palaces which await the faithful in the hereafter? For those radiant dwelling-places are fashioned from pure gold and lined with dazzling gems and glowing pearls. There, the unearthly and ethereal roses of heavenly delight never fade nor wither; the lush forests of perpetual verdure never lose their foliage nor dry up; the emerald meadows flow continually with golden rivers of honey, and the delicately resplendent crocus flowers give forth rare fragrances which never cease to enchant. The very breezes which blow are replete with the nectar of never-ending youth and vigor.

"And a splendid light bathes all things there in its ineffable refulgence, and the eye delights forever in an eternal and timeless day. Never does a cloud or shadow darken the pure and radiant serenity of the azure sky. Indeed, there is naught at all which disturbs the enjoyment of the infinite delights which abound. There is not the slightest trace of worry, anxiety, nor the smallest hint of care or sorrow. There is nothing there which is foul, fetid, or fearsome. The eye will perceive nothing that is ugly or ill-shapen or sordid. Rather, perfect and inexpressible beauty colors all things, and a glowing splendor suffuses the air itself. And everything that is there is made delightful by an inconceivable elegance.

"Nor is there anything which would offend the sense of hearing. On the contrary, there is heard always the ceaseless and ever-varying hymns of the angels and archangels which they sound to the glory of the King of heaven in iridescent harmonies of jubilation. No hint of bitterness or harshness is to be found, and thunder and lightning, storm and gales are never to be perceived. And all the plants give forth the flavor of rare spices, and the very air itself is infused with the delectable taste of cinnamon and wild honey. In short, the senses of vision, hearing, and taste are constantly filled with the richest pleasures and delights. And anything at all which the heart can imagine or desire is instantly granted to it!"

Thus ended Sebastian's wonderful description of the joys of paradise. And his words spoke the truth, presented in images and languages comprehensible to the senses. For the whole multitude of limitations which in this present world deprive us of the fulfilment of our souls' deepest desires will be utterly removed in heaven. Then the kindly Creator shall grant all good things freely and in abundance, with the alacrity and generosity of Divine grace. For, indeed, God created humankind so that we might possess life to the full. Yet he also placed death near the door of all our pleasures for as long as we inhabit this earthly realm. But whoever is freed from the fear of earthly death will attain to eternal and true life.

Once the parents and wives of Marcus and Marcellianus had heard all about the joys of heaven from Sebastian, they were astounded and filled with great longing. They asked him if those who attained admission to this celestial kingdom would still be subject to old age and death. How delighted they were to learn from him that the life-to-come was not only replete with all glory and joy but also lasted forever and ever!

Finally, to clarify what he had told them, they asked Sebastian whether it was really true that an eternity of pain and torment awaited the wicked and unbelievers after death and that unending joys awaited the just. And he assured them that it was indeed precisely so.

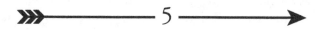

HAVING HEARD THIS wonderful description of the joys of heaven, Sebastian's hearers were all filled with wonder. Nevertheless, a certain question sprang up in their minds. And thus they asked, "We know that according to the law of Christ, worldly riches are to be treated with disdain and not sought after with eagerness. But why should this be, since they were made by the Creator God, Who made all things which exist—beasts and birds and reptiles alike. And this same Creator also placed within human beings the carnal desires and urgings of the flesh, and gave us all the delights which accompany them. Why should this Creator then declare them to be sins, and not only this, but also prepare an eternal fire for those who pursue such things?"

Sebastian carefully considered this profound philosophical conundrum, then replied, "Yes, all the good and delightful things of this life are truly the work of the Creator. Yet human beings are often led astray by them. For these created goods, such as riches and pleasure, say to our hearts, 'Love us so that we shall never be separated!' But this is a lie, for such created things are inconstant and unfaithful lovers. Even if one possesses them throughout one's mortal life (which is difficult and unlikely), we will inevitably lose them with death. Thus the pleasures and security they seem to offer are merely illusions.

"My friends, consider the case of the businessman or moneylender who will lend to one of his neighbors a piece of gold and then demand back two in return. Or consider the farmer who sows grain in the field in order to obtain a hundred times as much grain when he harvests the crop. Now, if the borrower is able to pay back the gold doubled and the earth is able to return the grain one-hundredfold to the farmer, shall not God also pay back to you anything you offer Him multiplied many times over? If you give up earthly wealth and carnal pleasures for the sake of glorifying and serving God, do you doubt that God will pay you back with better things many times over?

"But you may perhaps ask, 'Why has the Lord given me riches if He wants me to offer them back to Him?' God has given you the good things of this earth so that you may experience a certain small foretaste of rest, pleasure, happiness, and delight. In this way, you become acquainted with, and come to desire and aspire to, the true and eternal good things, which are found perfectly in heaven alone. And for the sake of these eternal and infinite blessings, all the good things of earth—which are but fleeting and limited reflections or anticipations of the good things of heaven—are to be offered freely to the Lord and not clung to as if they will last forever!

"If you do not believe me when I say this, I ask you to reflect a little on what happens to all the pleasures and delights of this mortal life. Either gluttony or greed invades and spoils them or the fires of lust pollute and disturb them. Thus the happiness which they seem to promise becomes instead a source of suffering and sorrow. And, what is more, death itself will eventually seize them all away from you, wrenching them from your grasp, no matter how much you may be attached to them! And then, what shall become of all your earthly riches and all your carnal pleasures? Truly, you will neither possess them, nor behold them, nor enjoy them ever again.

"Similarly, you may imagine that you are making a journey on foot, and that you happen to find yourself passing through a field of war, where a fierce battle is raging. Now imagine that as you travel, you are carrying with you a sack filled with treasures. As you make your way, arrows and spears are flying all around you and the treasures which you carry make you a particular target for attacks. But you meet a certain friend of yours who cares deeply about you. This friend is a very strong man and a mighty warrior—he's utterly invincible, in fact. And he says to you, 'Give me your sack of treasure, and I'll take care of it for you and give it back to you when this battle is over. And I'll also guard and protect you so that you may make your journey through all these perils unharmed!' Would you not gladly accept his kind and opportune offer?

"Now, the battlefield in the situation I have described is like our mortal life on this earth, and the sack filled with treasures you are carrying are all the riches of this world. The mighty warrior who offers to help and protect you, and who promises to repay you, is, of course, Christ. In Him you have an unassailable guardian in the fierce battle of this mortal life!

"But let us now come to the question of pleasure and delights. Listen carefully, my friends, to what all earthly delights are really telling you. For they are saying, 'If you really like us and enjoy our company, then entrust us to that One Who can keep us safe from the assaults of danger and decay, and Who will transport us to that realm where we shall flourish in fullness forever! For it is in that realm alone that you shall enjoy us completely and eternally. But if you insist on grasping us to yourselves in the here-and-now, and try to indulge in pleasures in this passing world of dust and shadow, you must know that we shall never bring you any lasting happiness or pleasure, and, indeed, we shall not serve you, but rather we shall make you into our servant and slave!' Thus it is that the pleasures we find in this mortal life all urge us to forgo them in the present world so that we may enjoy them for all eternity in heaven.

"Hence it is that we find written in Scripture, 'On account of the elect, our days will be shortened so that our servitude may not be prolonged.'[4] Let us pass through our service in this world without delay. In this world, we often are compelled to endure things which are burdensome, difficult, unpleasant, and futile. We do not participate in such things because we desire them or enjoy them but rather for the sake of Him Who has decreed that we be subject to them for a time.[5] Nevertheless, we shall, in due

---

[4] Matthew 24:22.

[5] See Romans 8:20.

course, certainly be liberated from the servitude of corruption and recalled to the glorious liberty of the children of God! Thus all pleasures and delights which we renounce or forgo in this world are not lost but rather stored up for us in the future life. In some ways, these earthly pleasures which we willingly forgo may be compared to treasures buried safely in the earth. The more they are hidden away and left untouched during the course of this present life, the more safely and securely are they being preserved for us in the life-to-come.

"My friends, let all your treasures be stored away safely for your eternal enjoyment in heaven rather than used up and lost in the present passing world, which shall soon disappear as smoke and shadows! But everything you possess in heaven shall continue to delight you forevermore, for ages without end. The wealth and delights you store up there shall never be exhausted, no matter how much you use them. Consider that this present life has a definite and inescapable limit. No human can realistically hope to live, at the very best, for much more than a hundred years. Then this present life shall be no more, and all its enjoyments and achievements, as well as its struggles and sufferings, will not only no longer *be* but be as if they had *never* been at all. They will be no more substantial than the memory of the shadow of a guest who visited us for one day then departed forever!

"But the life to come is quite different, for it will last eternally. The life of heaven shall be, as it were, constantly renewed in its youthfulness and vigor and will never grow old or tired. Like a circle, whose ending is identical with its beginning, the life-to-come will have no termination or finish. Surely, whoever is not filled with a desire for this glorious and endless life must be an utter wretch and a most pitiful degenerate! For fatuous and weak indeed is the one who fears to be separated from this brief and imperfect mortal life, with its many trials, vexations, and vanities and whose joys and pleasures are all fleeting and deceptive. And dull and foolish is the one whose heart does not aspire to the eternal life whose joys have neither limit nor end!

"And the person who for some reason chooses not to desire the wonderful eternal life which is to come will not only lose that splendid reward but, what is worse, shall find themselves made the captive of everlasting death. In that condition of everlasting death, there will burn fierce fires which are never extinguished. There will be tribulations which never cease and punishments which never reach an end. The infernal realm which those condemned to this perpetual torment inhabit is populated by foul demons and fallen angels, whose limbs are like the heads of dragons, whose eyes send forth a malignant and caustic glare like burning arrows, whose teeth are like the tusks of rabid elephants. These denizens of hell shall constantly inflict pain upon the damned, stinging them like the tails of scorpions. There, voices will be like the roar of ferocious lions, and their hideous visages will strike terror, pain, and deathlike despair into the hearts of all who behold them.

"Those condemned to this kingdom of endless torment and perpetual pain shall desperately long for death, but it shall never come. Rather, the soul who finds itself in this wretched state shall continue thus forever, like one who is painfully bitten by a serpent only to be bitten again and again and again for all eternity!"

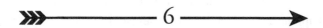

6

[AT THIS POINT in his discourse, Sebastian paused briefly to collect his thoughts and allow his hearers to reflect upon them. He then raised his eyes once more to the parents, wives, and children of Marcus and Marcellianus and resumed his discourse, continuing thus:]

"My friends, such are the reasons for the battle in which Marcus and Marcellianus have now so bravely entered. Such are the considerations which equip their souls to embrace the pains of holy martyrdom.

"O loving parents and wives of these most noble saints, do not try now to call them back from the glory of the eternal life into which they shall soon depart! Do not try to drag them from this wonderful life to the realm of unending death; do not try to remove them from the light to consign them to darkness; do not try to take them from the kingdom of eternal rest to hand them over to perpetual pain!

"For to do so would be to make yourselves allies to the devil, as he tries to enmesh souls with his deceptions and temptations as a cunning fisherman trying to capture fish in a net. For it is the practice of this nefarious tempter to offer the bait of momentary and passing sweetness and delight, but in which is hidden bitter punishments and lethal torments. For how better may one describe the situation for the soul who is lured away from the eternal happiness of heaven by the passing and transient joys of this mortal life, which flees like a shadow and disappears like a dream?

"Very rightly do we look with disdain upon those weak characters who commit some crime for the sake of a momentary pleasure or thrill and then find themselves condemned to undergo the punishment of torture and death in some public arena. Yet those who condemn their own immortal souls to damnation for the sake of earthly happiness may be compared to such foolish and feeble characters, for they have done the exact same thing!

"Yes, it is in accordance with the counsels of the devil that weak-minded criminals lose their lives to gain some momentary pleasure. But it is similar counsel which you are now offering Marcus and Marcellianus, your sons and your husbands, when you seek to deter them from glorious martyrdom. For you would urge them to lose the priceless treasure of eternal life and blessedness simply to gain a few more days upon this troubled earth, and, what is worse, for the sake of these few extra days of earthly life, you would then have them undergo torments which know no end in the world-to-come!

"Perhaps you may still object, and ask 'But why should a true Christian not fear pains and tortures during this present life? Indeed, if, as you say, we are to fear everlasting torments in the next life, should we not also fear torments in the here-and-now?' To this I respond that if a person knows that by accepting a single moment of pain, he shall rejoice forever in infinite delight, then any fear or hesitation he may have felt about the momentary pain will be utterly dispelled. And, conversely, if a person fears any earthly executioner or torturer, should he not be filled with an infinitely greater terror at the threat of the incomparably worse and longer-lasting punishments which await in hell?

"For which are more greatly to be feared, I ask you? Should we fear most greatly those tribulations which are here today and gone tomorrow, those fires which burn today and by tomorrow will be extinguished, those pains which spring up for a brief hour and within the same hour have passed? Or should we not rather fear much more those tribulations which *never* end, the fire which shall *never* be extinguished, and the pains which will continue without relief for endless ages? For the pains of this present life are either tolerable and able to be endured or, if they are not able to be endured, they are very soon finished by death itself.[6] But the pains of hell, in contrast, are more intense than any and all forms of earthly torture, and not only this but they endure forever and ever, with no hope of cessation. Indeed, they are constantly renewed, like a fire that, once lit, burns ever more intensely.

---

[6] This is a quotation of a well-known saying attributed to the Greek philosopher Epicurus, "All pain is either bearable or short-lived." It was quoted by Marcus Aurelius in his *Meditations* and by Seneca in his *Moral Epistles* and seems to have been a popular observations amongst the Stoics of Rome.

"Let us therefore urge anyone whom we truly love to do all they can to escape such horrors and torments! And let us also prepare ourselves strongly so that we may be free of them. Let us not fear to endure one hour's worth of pain in our physical bodies so that we may merit to enjoy eternal bliss in the future with Christ! Let us arm ourselves with courage so that when our soul departs from its mortal coil, it may bear with it the glorious palm of martyrdom and hasten, triumphant and free, to the star-filled and celestial realms of eternal delight.

"May our tears be turned into rejoicing, for we ought not to mourn as if our friends were about to die but rather congratulate them as honored victors who are very soon to reign forever with Christ, the King of the Universe! We should applaud for them as warriors who have conquered their foes, and trampled their adversaries under their feet. For, behold, the day is at hand when the diabolical enemy, who erroneously believes himself to have defeated Marcus and Marcellianus, will be defeated by them. He, the wicked devil, believes he has taken them captive; yet it is he who shall be held in chains. He believes that he mocks and insults them, yet it is he who is mocked by them. He believes that he strangles them when it is he himself who is being strangled and overthrown!

"In facing persecutions, it behooves us to open the eyes of our souls, like a person aroused from deep slumber. Then we will perceive clearly all the snares which the devil has laid for us, and yet which we have so fortunately escaped, thanks to the grace and mercy of almighty God! Rather, it is the devil himself and all his wicked henchmen who have fallen into the pits which they themselves have dug. And when we witness this marvelous thing, we may very fittingly sing the words of the psalm:

> *My foes have dug a pit for me*
> *To catch me as their prey,*
> *Yet they themselves in it did fall,*
> *Yea, fallen now are they!"*[7]

---

[7] See Psalm 56:7.

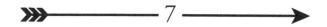 7

WHILST ALL OF these wonderful counsels flowed forth from the mouth of Sebastian, the saint was clad in a simple tunic and girt with a leather belt. But suddenly, as if illuminated by the Holy Spirit, a glowing radiance shone all about him, as if descending from the very vault of heaven. Seven glorious angels then appeared and robed him in a luminous pallium of celestial brilliance. At the same time, a young man of remarkably handsome appearance and suffused with the majesty and splendor of the Divinity itself appeared at his side.[8] He offered to Sebastian a sign of peace and said, "Thou art with Me always!"

All of these things took place within the house of a certain imperial magistrate by the name of Nicostratus. For it was in the villa of this Nicostratus that Marcus and Marcellianus were being

---

[8] This young man is evidently understood to be Christ Himself.

held under arrest.[9] Now, Nicostratus had a wife called Zoe. This Zoe had suffered from a severe illness six years before, which had taken her voice away completely and left her mute. But despite being mute, she retained her faculty of hearing; in fact, if anything, this had become more acute and sensitive than before.

Thanks to this, she had overheard everything which Sebastian had said about heaven and hell and eternal life, and had also seen him become illuminated by the miraculous light. Zoe was completely convinced of the truth of Sebastian's words, as her heart was filled with the grace of faith. She fell on her knees before the saint. Although she could not speak, she attempted to communicate with him her joy at her newfound belief by means of hand gestures. After a little while, Sebastian realized that she was unable to use her voice and enquired as to the cause. He was informed that due to an illness some years ago, she had been completely deprived of the faculty of speech.

Upon hearing this, he raised his eyes to heaven and, in a clear voice, uttered the following prayer, "If I am a true servant of Christ, and if all the things I have spoken of and which this woman has believed are true, then may my Lord Jesus Christ return to her the use of her voice; may He open her mouth now just as He once opened the mouth of the mute Zechariah!"[10]

---

[9] The keeping of Marcus and Marcellianus in custody in the house of an official, rather than a common prison, reflects the fact that they were of a wealthy and illustrious family and that the Roman officials were therefore particularly desirous to have them abandon their Christian faith so as to avoid the necessity of executing them. This is explained by Nicostratus in chapter 11.

[10] See Luke 1:64.

And, as he said these words, Sebastian made the sign of the cross over her mouth. And at once Zoe's voice was restored to her, and she spoke in a loud and clear tone. She said, "Blessed are you, and blessed are the gracious words which have issued from your mouth! And most truly blessed are all those who believe in Christ, the Son of the living God. For as you were speaking, I perceived with my own eyes an angel descending from heaven to you and holding a book open before your eyes. And it was from this book that you read as you spoke of the wonderful truths of eternal life. Blessed indeed are all those who believe the great mysteries you have uttered and the Divine truths which you have so nobly expressed!"

All were amazed to behold Zoe, who had been unable to articulate a single word for so long, now using her voice so freely and speaking with such eloquence and fluency. She continued thus, "And cursed are all those who doubt the glorious verities which you have pronounced and refuse to accept their manifest truth. For just as the golden light of dawn dispels the darkness of night, even so has your speech dispelled the darkness of error and illuminated the night of blind ignorance. Yes, indeed! For now the serene day of faith and of truth has arisen in my heart. For me you have not only freed me from the murky blackness of pagan superstition in which I was enshrouded but have also opened the door of my mouth and restored to me the faculty of speech, of which I had been deprived for six long and difficult years!"

When Nicostratus, Zoe's husband, witnessed what had taken place, he was astounded. He too recognized the power of Christ working through Sebastian, which had manifested itself in such a marvelous and merciful manner. He fell to his knees before Sebastian, as well as before Marcus and Marcellianus, and entreated their forgiveness for having held them as prisoners upon the wicked commands of the tyrannical emperor. He instantly unfastened the chains which held them and embraced them affectionately. He also implored them to go free from his custody. "If I am punished for releasing you in this way," said he, "then I shall consider myself to be truly blessed! Indeed, if the death sentence is imposed upon me for my violation of the imperial commands, then perhaps my own blood will wash away the dark stains of my guilt. In this way, by the mercy of God, I may hopefully evade the torments of perpetual damnation of which you have so eloquently spoken and attain to the glory of eternal life which God has made manifest through your inspired mouth, O blessed Sebastian!"

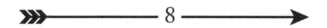

8

WHEN NICOSTRATUS URGED Marcus and Marcellianus to depart freely from their captivity and escape, the holy twins refused adamantly. "If you, who have only just now accepted the gift of faith, cling to it with such enthusiasm and determination, how shall we—who have been imbued with the same faith since our infancy—now flee from it like craven cowards? Shall we disdain to drink of the glorious chalice of martyrdom which the Lord has given to us and instead hand it over to you?

"Truly, Christ is rich and generous in all good things. He bestows His blessings and graces with a liberality and abundance which exceeds anything for which we could ask or hope. Indeed, while you were still laboring under the delusion of unbelief, He freely gave to you the splendid light of truth. How much more He shall give to you now that you have embraced the faith! Shall He not grant you whatever you ask of Him in His most holy Name? For the Divine Mercy is always prepared to give of its infinite abundance without reserve and without stinting. And it never ceases to multiply the gifts of grace which it has bestowed so that the minds and hearts of the faithful are constantly drawn to the penetration of more sublime and more wonderful mysteries!

"Your faith has only now just begun, thanks to the gift of the heavenly Teacher. Through this faith, you have gained within the space of an hour such treasures of wisdom which can barely be attained through years of philosophical study and intellectual reflection. For you, unlike us, are not held back by attachments and responsibilities to elderly parents, nor are you bound to this passing world by tender affections towards young children you have begotten.[11] Blest be God, for you have in an instant abandoned your attachment to the vain things of this earthly life, which for so many years you blindly loved and served. You have stepped out courageously upon unknown paths to arrive at the salvation offered by Christ. In your souls, you yearn for the eternal delights of heaven and are filled with disdain for transient honors and pleasure.

"What a wonderful herald this sudden conversion is for your future sanctity and fidelity! What a marvelous example of virtue! For you have not yet been consecrated to Christ through the sacramental waters of baptism, nor undergone the training of the catechumenate; yet already you are willing to fight and to die in the battle for the faith. Yes, for the immortal King of heaven, you would take up the glorious arms of virtue. For you desire to set us, who are committed soldiers of Christ, free from our chains.

---

[11] Evidently, Nicostratus and Zoe did not have any offspring.

And you desire to risk death yourselves for the sake of granting freedom to us, who are already condemned and destined to shed our blood for the omnipotent Monarch of the Universe!"

At this, all who were present—the parents and wives of Marcus and Marcellianus, as well as the servants of the household of Nicostratus and Zoe—began to weep, filled with awe at the power of holy conversion and penitence. Then Marcus addressed his parents, as well as his wife and the wife of his brother. He spoke thus, "O my beloved father and mother, and you, our dearest wives; hearken to my words! Learn to fight boldly against the attacks of the devil. Gird yourself with the shield of all virtue to ward of the envenomed arrows of fleshly desire and the deceptive snares of carnal affection. Enter boldly into the battle against the manifold forces of the malign foe. Fight with all your hearts and stand your ground with constancy so that you may enter into the radiant glory of the Deity! For the minions of Lucifer and the earthly agents of the devil will constantly assail you and try to harm and mislead you. But, even though they may inflict passing suffering upon your physical body, these fiends are utterly powerless to conquer the soul which is armed by strong faith in the Lord Christ.

"Truly, soldiers are rendered more glorious and honorable on account of any wounds and scars which they have acquired in battle for their King. It is for this and no other reason that the devil is permitted by God to wage his war against us. Hence he now attacks us with his fury, through which he vainly imagines himself to be able to wrestle from us our heavenly reward.

He inflicts torments upon us so that his wicked hopes are not thwarted. He threatens death so that he may terrify the weak.

"Yet this wicked tempter also sometimes promises us life and well-being, but only so that he can snatch true life and genuine salvation away from us. He sometimes promises false security and safety, but only so that he can destroy our real and lasting peace. He employs every possible deception and all the cunning ploys of war against us, offering to rescue our physical bodies from the torments and pains which pass, but only so that he can subject our immortal souls to thralldom to vice and bind our hearts with the oppressive chains of sin!

"But may we strive not to succumb to the attacks and tricks of this malign foe. Let us be ready to suffer and die in the body in order that we may save our immortal souls! Why should we Christians—who are made into strong warriors by the weapons of faith and virtue—surrender in this war against the devil when we are fully capable of being victorious? Why should we fear earthly death when we realize that this is something natural and unavoidable—that it is merely an inevitable and necessary part of our mortal life and not a punishment or an evil? Why, I say, should we fear the death in the here-and-now when we know this earthly life to be but a fleeting and illusory shadow and our real and eternal life to be found in heaven?

"For surely we must perceive that those who give themselves to the service of the things of this passing life serve an inconstant and capricious mistress, who is barely able to govern herself! How many calamities and misfortunes fall upon those who seek their treasures in the deceptive and unstable theatre of the present world—such people are prey to sudden ruin, to random disasters, to sickness and fever, to lightning bolts from heaven, to shipwrecks, to blows from the sword, and to all the thousand mischances and accidents of chaos and of fate! And all these things happen, not because some torturer inflicts them as punishments, but through the mere caprices of chance.

"My brothers and sisters, it is far wiser to offer our services and loyalty not to the untrustworthy mistress of this world but rather to the faithful and true Lord, the immortal and only God. It is far more prudent and profitable to set our hopes not upon the deceptive, short-lived, and unstable things of this passing world but rather upon the life of eternal glory which awaits us in heaven, where all pain and suffering shall be left far behind!"

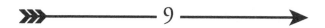

9

WHEN MARCUS HAD finished his discourse, saying the words recorded in the previous chapter as well as many other similarly inspiring and wise exhortations, all those who were present began to give praise and glory to God and to weep with tears of sincere emotion. For they were all deeply touched by the heroic determination of the two young men, Marcus and Marcellianus, to undergo martyrdom for the love of Christ and for the sake of gaining eternal life. Indeed, even the imperial officers who were present in order to convince the two saints to renounce their faith and worship the gods of Rome were thoroughly convinced by all they had heard and witnessed. Nicostratus then spoke up in tones of firm resolution, "As God is my witness, I hereby vow that I shall taste neither food nor drink until I have been initiated into the mysteries of the Christian religion!"

Upon hearing this, Saint Sebastian was filled with delight. "I congratulate you on your wisdom, Sir," he said. "Change now the honor which you possess for a better one, and exchange the service in which you are now enrolled for something infinitely superior. Cease to be an officer of the emperor, and become instead an officer of God! Assemble together all those whom you hold in custody, as well as all those here present, who wish to be initiated into the divine mysteries of our religion. Then let us go to one of the holy priests of God so that all may receive the saving sacrament of Baptism. For we know that the wicked devil is constantly striving to steal human souls away from God. How much more then ought we endeavor to release souls from their captivity to the devil and the world and restore them to their Creator!"

When he heard this, a question arose in the mind of Nicostratus. "But many of these people have lived wicked or sinful lives, and their hearts and souls are deeply stained with iniquity and guilt. How is it possible for such persons to receive the holy sacrament of which you speak and to be initiated into the celestial and sublime mysteries of your faith?"

To this Sebastian responded, "Our Savior came into this world for the very purpose of taking sins away, and He has deigned to reveal the mysteries of our salvation. For He Himself became the sacrifice which washed human iniquity away. He Himself is the Redeemer Who breaks the chains of sin! If you undertake this work for the sake of Christ—both accepting baptism yourself and leading all of these now present to the same saving sacrament—be assured that He shall not fail to reward you. For you shall win for yourself the glorious crown of martyrdom, a crown which blossoms with the wonderful flower of imperishable radiance and which bears the fruit of eternal life."

Encouraged by these words, Nicostratus then ordered his chief officer and lieutenant, a trustworthy man called Claudius, to assemble together all those held in custody, as well as all members of his household who were interested in the wonderful truths which Sebastian had spoken.

When this had been done, the assembled group all stood before Sebastian, those being held in custody still bearing their chains. And the saint addressed them thus, "The wickedness of the devil is destined to be defeated always by the power of God! Each of you has now a special and privileged opportunity of being freed from your sins and from unending punishment and death, and being called from the passing and illusory joys of this earthly life and entering into the eternal glory of heaven.

"Your own experience of life has surely taught you that the wicked devil—the ruler of this world—tirelessly seeks to overturn people of virtue and good morals and to submerge them in the muddy swamp of sin and corruption. It is against this devil that we are now called to do battle! For although you were once enslaved by his temptations and deceptions, I now call you to return to your true Creator and the God Who loves you, through the holy sacraments of the Christian faith.

"Turn away from the devil! For he is not your master, nor your creator, nor your father. It is the immortal God of heaven Who is your Father and Lord and Creator. Leave Satan behind! For he seeks only to lead you to share with him in his own eternal punishment; all his promises are false and all his temptations are deceptions. Does it not behoove you to turn earnestly to the omnipotent God, Who, in His fathomless mercy, handed over His only-begotten Son to death so that you might be redeemed from everlasting death and saved from the fires of unending torment?"

Once Sebastian had completed this eloquent exhortation, all those who were present were moved to the deepest emotion and most heartfelt compunction. Falling to their knees, tears flowed forth from their eyes in abundant streams. Wordless sighs of penitence and sorrow, combined with holy and celestial yearnings, poured forth from their lips. And they unanimously proclaimed themselves to desire initiation into the mysteries of Christian faith through the sacrament of Baptism.

So Sebastian commanded that the prisoners be released from their chains and urged all of them to wait patiently for him to organize all that was necessary for this to take place.

10

AFTER THIS, SEBASTIAN promptly went off to see Polycarp, a certain holy priest whom he knew. Now this Polycarp was in hiding at the time, on account of the persecutions taking place in Rome, but Sebastian was a close friend of his and knew where he could be found. After greeting him, the saint narrated to him all that had transpired and told him about the mass conversion which had taken place as a result of the courageous witness of Marcus and Marcellianus. He asked Polycarp if he would agree to accompany him to the palace of Nicostratus and there to administer the sacrament of Baptism to the new converts.

Polycarp was filled with joy and wonder and gave thanks to God for His gracious mercy in performing this marvelous thing. He gladly agreed to accompany Sebastian, and together they returned to the residence of Nicostratus. Polycarp greeted all those present warmly with the following words, "My brothers and sisters, you are indeed blessed! For you have heard the words of our Lord and Savior, who said, 'Come unto Me, all ye who are weary and heavily burdened, and I shall give you rest. Take My yoke upon your shoulders, and learn from Me—for I am meek and humble of heart. And ye shall find rest for your souls.'[12]

"My brothers and sisters, you have not yet been washed by the sacramental waters of Baptism and thus made adopted children of God. Indeed, it was not very long ago that some of you even sought to retract the holy brothers, Marcus and Marcellianus, from their faith. But now, through the grace of God and the action of penitence, you are filled with a desire to embrace that very same saving faith. A little while ago, you wished to deter these brothers from the suffering of their impending martyrdom, yet now you yourselves eagerly desire this very same destiny, for you realize that it carries with it a splendid palm of victory and a crown of imperishable glory.

"Indeed, this is often the way of things with Christ. For He transformed Saul, who had been a vitriolic persecutor of Christians, into Saint Paul, the great proclaimer of the Gospel. He created an apostle from an apostate, and changed a persecutor of the Church into a teacher of the same Church. He who had formerly rejoiced to see others suffer for their Christian faith came to rejoice to accept sufferings himself for the holy name of Christ.

"The same God who created an apostle out of a persecutor of the Church shall now save your own souls from the torments of hell and liberate you from your thralldom to the ancient drag-

---

[12] Matthew 11:28–29.

on! He will lead you from the darkness of falsehood to the glorious light of truth and shall open wide for you the glowing doors to eternal life! And the legions of demons, who are the creatures of darkness, will be greatly grieved at this, but the angels of light shall exult over you with untold joy!

"Let each one of you who has been inspired to seek the saving sacrament of Baptism come forward and give to me your name as a candidate. And each one must fast now for the remainder of the day. Tomorrow you will all be baptized and enter into the number of the chosen of Christ! Truly it is fitting that you who have resolved to cast off the filth of this world and all its impure desires should be washed to radiant splendor in the sacramental waters of Baptism. Then, with your souls robed in the white garments of innocence, you shall hasten to your true Lord and King, Christ."

With these and similar words, Polycarp encouraged all those present. They all were filled with joy and eager to enroll as candidates for Baptism.

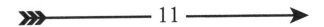

11

WHEN ALL THIS had happened, Claudius (the trusted officer of Nicostratus) went to his master and said, "Master, you should know that the prefect, Chromatius,[13] has been advised that you ordered Marcus and Marcellianus to be taken into custody in your own villa. He is perplexed by this and would like an explanation from you about why you did this. Take good care that you answer him prudently!"

And so Nicostratus went to the palace of Chromatius, the prefect,[14] and was admitted to his presence. Chromatius asked him why he had ordered Marcus and Marcellianus to be held at his own villa rather than the imperial prison. To this, Nicostratus responded, "Your Excellency, I did this so as to stir up terror in

---

[13] The name of the prefect, Chromatius, is not given at this point in the Latin and appears only in the next chapter. However, since it seems to be the same person, his name has been added here for the sake of clarity.

[14] The prefect of Rome was an important official, responsible for maintaining law and order in the city.

the hearts of these two young men so that they might repent from their errors and abandon the Christian faith. As you know, I have a large number of prisoners being held at my villa who are undergoing tortures or awaiting execution. I believed that by seeing these people, Marcus and Marcellianus would be filled with fear." [Indeed, Nicostratus had spoken honestly in replying thus to the prefect, for this had, in fact, been his original intention in having the young men detained at his villa.]

The prefect was perfectly satisfied with this explanation and very pleased with Nicostratus's plan. He assured him that if he managed to induce Marcus and Marcellianus to renounce Christianity and avoid execution, he could expect a generous reward since their parents were extremely wealthy.

Nicostratus then returned to his villa accompanied by Claudius. As they walked, Nicostratus related to Claudius all that had happened. He told him about Sebastian and how he was a favorite of the emperor, yet also a faithful Christian. He repeated the eloquent and inspiring words of exhortation Sebastian had said, expressing so convincingly the fleeting and ephemeral nature of all earthly things and describing the everlasting glory of bliss of the eternal life of heaven. Nicostratus also told Claudius about how Sebastian had been illuminated by a miraculous light as he spoke, and how he had cured his wife from her condition of being mute which had lasted for six years.

When Claudius heard this, he was filled with astonishment. He fell to the feet of Nicostratus and exclaimed, "O master, you know that I myself have two young sons, who were borne to me by my beloved wife, who—alas!—is now dead. Both of my young sons, [Felicissimus and Felix], are badly afflicted with ill health. The elder of them is all swollen with fluid retention, and the younger one is covered with a terrible rash.[15] I ask that you permit me to take these sons of mine to this Sebastian whom you have told me about. For I am sure that if he was able to cure your wife of her long-enduring muteness and restore to her the faculty of speech, he shall easily be able to cure my two sons of their afflictions!"

To this request, Nicostratus very willingly agreed. And so Claudius returned to his house and collected his two boys and took them to the villa of Nicostratus, where Sebastian was still present. Leading them before the saint, he said, "Most noble Sebastian, there is no shadow of doubt left in my heart; I firmly believe that Christ, Whom you worship, is the true God! I bring to you my two offspring, as you can see, in the hope that you might be able to cure them from their affliction and sufferings and guard them against the peril of death which threatens them."

All those who were present then applauded joyfully when they heard this statement of faith. And they declared that all of them who had been suffering from any illness of debility had that day been cured as soon as they had accepted Christ as their Lord and God. Claudius said that he, too, fervently wished to become a Christian.

Upon hearing these things, the priest Polycarp renewed his instruction that all of those wishing to be baptized the next day should come forth and give him their names. The first to give

---

[15] The Latin text states that his son was *"diversis vulneribus oppressus,"* literally "oppressed by various wounds." It seems likely that this is referring to a rash of some kind.

his name was Tranquillinus, the father of Marcus and Marcellianus. After this, six friends of the two young men came forward, Ariston, Crescentianus, Eutychianus, Urban, Vitalia, and Justus. After this came Nicostratus (the owner of the villa), his brother Castor, and Claudius. Next came the two young sons of Claudius, Felicissimus and Felix.

After these followed Marcia, the mother of Marcus and Marcellianus, together with their wives and children. Then came Symphorosa, the wife of Claudius,[16] and Zoe, the wife of Nicostratus. Also, the entire household of Nicostratus, consisting of some thirty-three men and women, presented themselves as candidates for baptism. And all of the other persons who were being held in custody in the villa (sixteen altogether) also enrolled.

Thus it was that a total of sixty-three were enrolled for baptism. And the next day, they were all baptized by Polycarp. Sebastian himself acted as the sponsor for all the men and boys, and two pious matrons, Beatrix and Lucina, acted as sponsors for the women and girls. The first to be baptized were the two sons of Claudius. And as soon as they were washed with the sacramental waters and the name of the most Holy Trinity was spoken over them, all signs of their previous afflictions disappeared completely!

After these children, Tranquillinus came forward to be baptized. Now Tranquillinus was an elderly man and suffered from chronic gout. This gout was so severe that he could barely stand upright or move about without assistance. He began to remove

---

[16] As it was mentioned that the mother of the two sons of Claudius had passed away, this Symphrosa must be a second wife to Claudius.

his outer garment to prepare for baptism, but as he did so, he felt searing pains in his joints. He apologized for his slowness, explaining that it was unbearable torture for him to try to move his body in this way. Polycarp then questioned him, saying, "Tranquillinus, do you believe that Jesus Christ, the only-begotten Son of God, is able to confer healing and salvation upon you? Do you believe that this same Jesus Christ is able to take away all your sins? If you do believe this will all your heart, declare it now with the words of your mouth!"

Tranquillinus responded, "I do so believe! There is nothing I seek or desire other than forgiveness for my sins. Even though my physical pains may continue after I have received the sanctification of holy baptism, never shall I doubt the faith which I now profess in Jesus Christ. Yes, I truly believe Him to be the only Son of God, Who is able to confer health and healing to bodies and minds, and Who is able to lead the dead forth into the glories of eternal life!"

When Tranquillinus had made this stirring profession of faith in a loud and resolute voice, all those who were present shed tears of pure joy, and they all implored the Lord that He should manifest to the old man the fitting rewards of his belief. As the priest Polycarp anointed him with the oil of chrism, he once more asked him solemnly if he believed in the Father, the Son, and the Holy Spirit. When the old man responded, "I believe!" the gout which had contorted and tormented his body was immediately dispelled. At once, he was able to stand upright unassisted and move about with the flexibility and ease of a young man. And as he entered into the baptismal pool, he exclaimed, "O Lord, You are the one God, living and true, Whom this miserable world has failed to recognize!"

After this, all were baptized in turn, in due order. For the next ten days and nights, they spent their time continuously giving praise and thanks to God in prayer and sacred songs. Indeed, they were all like faithful soldiers ready to give their very lives for the holy name of Christ. And even among the women and children, such noble courage burned in their hearts that they looked upon the prospect of cruel martyrdom without any trace of fear and trepidation as they prepared themselves to face the assaults and attacks of the wicked devil.

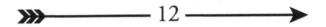 12

Shortly after the days of post-baptismal thanksgiving were completed, the prefect, Chromatius, summoned to himself Tranquillinus, the father of Marcellianis and Marcus. He enquired of him how he was and how his sons were faring in custody. To this, Tranquillinus responded, "Your Excellency, no words could suffice for me to thank you for the benefits you have conferred upon us. Unless you had passed sentence on my sons, they should have been lost to me, and my sons would have lost their father! All those who understand the feeling of paternal affection and love shall congratulate me on what has happened. Even Your Excellency must share my joy, for, thanks to you, those who were about to die are now going to receive true life, those who were oppressed by cares and sorrows will soon rejoice, and those who were in peril shall be brought into perfect safety!"

Now, it is to be noted that the prefect, Chromatius, completely misunderstood the significance of the words of Tranquillinus. For what Tranquillinus meant was that, thanks to the sentence of death passed upon his sons, they were soon to enter into the eternal life of heaven. But what Chromatius imagined that he was saying was that thanks to the opportunity he had given to the brothers to renounce their faith, they would be spared from mortal execution. So he said, "Tomorrow, let your sons burn some incense before the Roman gods as a sign of submission. And then you shall have them back, free and unharmed!"

But Tranquillinus responded, "Most illustrious sir, you seem to have misunderstood me. It is purely because my sons, and I myself also, bear the name of 'Christian' that we partake in the great blessings which I described to you. And this name is of such great strength that neither you nor anyone in this world shall ever overcome it!"

Upon hearing this, the prefect was shocked and angered. "Tranquillinus, you are insane!" But Tranquillinus answered, "I *was* insane. But by believing in Christ, I have cast off the insanity of pagan error and come to know the eternal truth."

Chromatius then exclaimed, "I perceive that not only have you failed to retract your sons from this superstitious falsehood but that they, on the contrary, have convinced you yourself with their error!" To this, Tranquillinus said, "Your Excellency, you are wrong to call it an 'error.' What you should call an error is the worship of idols. For this practice is what causes human beings to depart from the way of true life and to enter into the way of death!"

Chromatius enquired, "Pray tell, what is this 'way of death' of which you speak?" Tranquillinus explained, "Surely, the darkness of heathen superstition is the way of death. For you worship dead men, whom you believe to have been transformed into deities,[17] and you bow down before images of them fashioned from wood and stone."

The prefect was perplexed. "Are you saying that the deities we worship are not truly gods?" he enquired. Tranquillinus answered, "No, they are not gods! Consider the myths and stories which surround them, and how badly and dishonestly these so-called gods have lived and behaved! Do you think Jupiter to be truly capable of commanding thunder and lightning when he himself is ruled by malice and lust? Who is safe from such a being who is believed to have slaughtered his own father? And to what depth of depravity would he not descend since he took his own sister as his wife?[18] For in the forums, in the squares, in houses, and in every place, daily it is read that Juno, the natural sister of Jupiter, is also his wife. And even those who worship this Jupiter do not deny that he practices foul impurity with Ganymede, his servant boy!

"Distinguished sir, do you not err to regard such beings as gods? Should the Romans worship as deities characters who should be condemned for their sins and crimes? For the true God of heaven is abandoned, and yet people say to an object of stone, 'You are my god,' or to a carving of wood, 'Please help me!'"

---

[17] Many ancient authorities assert that the many of the gods of the Classical world were originally famous human beings whose memory was venerated after their death, and so eventually came to be worshiped as gods. See Wisdom 14:15-20.

[18] In Classical mythology, Jupiter is recounted as having killed and usurped his father, Saturn, and to have married his sister, Juno.

To this, Chromatius objected, "It is only since people have begun to abandon the old gods and the traditional sacrifices that Rome has been attacked and suffered devastations." But Tranqillinus answered him, "That is simply not true. For if you read diligently the histories of Rome written by Livy,[19] you will discover that before the advent of Christianity when everyone still burnt incense to Jove,[20] thirty thousand young men were once slaughtered in one single day. And it is well documented that Rome suffered from the scourge of famine and from innumerable devastating plagues long before Christianity and the worship of the true God of heaven were even known here.

But in our own times, when many Roman citizens have come to adore the one, true, and unseen God, now the empire enjoys unprecedented peace and prosperity. But what is deplorable is that this one true God, Who has brought such benefits to Rome, is not yet officially recognized by the authorities. Instead, the official institutions of the empire continue to worship created things instead of the Creator Himself!"

The prefect reflected upon these words for some time before raising another objection. "If we are to worship as a deity whatever or whoever it is who bestows the most generous benefits on humankind," he said, "then surely we should worship the sun. For it is the sun giving light and warmth to the earth which causes

---

[19] An ancient Roman historian.

[20] This seems to be a reference to the Roman defeat at Syphax in northern Africa, in which, according to Livy, thirty thousand Romans were slaughtered in a single battle against the Carthaginians. Tranquillinus mentions it here to refute the assertion of Chromatius that it is only since the advent of Christianity that Rome had begun to suffer disaster.

crops and plants of all kind to spring forth from the ground. There is nothing more useful to humankind than the light of the sun, by which we live, work, move about, and perceive the rest of the world. And the warmth and energy coming from the sun imparts rejuvenation and life to all terrestrial things."

To this argument, Tranquillinus responded, "This is an immense error! For if a rich man bestows benefits upon others, and does this through the agency of some servant of his, it would be infinite foolishness to give gratitude and honor to the servant rather than the rich man himself who sent the gift. To give another example, kings from foreign lands often send their choicest produce to Rome. They do this by engaging ships and employing sailors. Now, is it the ships and sailors who deserve thanks or is it not rather the kings who send the produce to whom gratitude is due? It is, of course, those who give the gifts, not those who merely act as the agents for their delivery!

"According to precisely the same principle, we ought to give gratitude solely to God, the Creator of all, rather than the elements of nature which act as His servants and agents. For truly, all things in this world and in the realm of nature are governed by His providence and power. It is at God's command that the sun sets each day, and at His command that it rises to bestow upon the blessing of each new day!"

# 13

THE INTEREST OF Chromatius was greatly aroused by the words of Tranquillinus. And so, he sought further clarification concerning the beliefs of the Christians. "If you worship this one, invisible God, as you say," he asked, "how is it that you also worship Christ, Who was put to death upon a cross?"

Tranquillinus responded, "This is a very astute question, and a necessary one if you are to understand our beliefs. For all those who have no desire to believe also have no desire to understand."

The prefect continued, "How is it that you claim that only the unseen God of heaven should be worshiped, the God whom no mortal senses can perceive nor human mind understand. And yet, you worship Christ as a deity. Now Christ was definitely seen and heard, and even had all of our human frailties, as is clearly shown in the narrative of His passion and death!"

Tranquillinus answered, "I shall answer this question by offering you a similitude. Imagine that you possessed a precious ring fashioned from pure gold and containing a rare gemstone. Now imagine that the same ring was somehow immersed in mud or dung. The precious ring may be likened to the human person, with the gold being the body and the gemstone being the soul. And the dung and mud in which it became immersed may be likened to the sin and vices to which our human nature has become enmeshed, with its multitude of wickedness, miseries, and woes.

"Now imagine that you sent some of your servants to retrieve this precious ring. But they are unable to do so, because the ring has sunken so deeply into the filth. So instead you decide to go forth yourself. But before you do, you remove your garments of fine silk and put on the coarse garbs of a peasant. This may be likened to God sending forth firstly His prophets. These, like the servants who were unable to recover the ring, could not convince humankind to turn away from sin. But when you yourself go forth clothed as a servant, this is like the incarnation of God, which took place in Christ. For in the coming of Christ, the eternal Word took off its celestial splendor, although it did not lose its divine nature. And it put on our humble humanity and entered into the misery of our mortal condition. It was by doing this that God was able to rescue our human nature from the filth of sin and woe in which it was immersed. Just as you would have rejoiced greatly to recover your precious ring, so did God rejoice to save our immortal humanity, fashioned in the image of God Himself!

"Now if you imagine that when you had removed your fine robes and put on the humble garb of a servant, and some of your own servants met you, would they refuse to acknowledge you as their lord and master simply because you were dressed like them? Certainly not! So it is pure foolishness to deny the divinity of Christ on account of His incarnation. Indeed, anyone who does so cannot possibly be saved from the fire of hell. But for those who do believe, we have been washed clean from the filth of sin by the waters of the sacrament of Baptism. And these same waters shall guard us from the inextinguishable flames of eternal torment!"

Chromatius replied, "I can see that you sincerely believe in all of these, Tranquillinus. I also have been told that you were healed of the severe gout which had afflicted you for so long through the virtue of the name of Christ, and I can see plainly that you are now in perfect health. Nevertheless, you should know that the fury of our invincible emperor, Diocletian, burns furiously against Christians. Are you really ready to confront that insatiable wrath?"

Tranquillinus affirmed that he was. "It is foolishness to fear the anger of a mortal and not to fear the wrath of God even more!" said he. The prefect assured him that they would soon continue their discussion and ordered him to be held in custody until then.

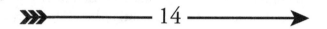

14

LATER THAT NIGHT, Chromatius secretly sent forth one of his officers to bring Tranquillinus to himself. He said to him, "As I mentioned, I realize that you have been healed from a very serious illness. You should know that I, too, suffer from such a disease. In fact, I am subject to the same painful condition of gout from which you have been cured. I promise you not only your freedom but also a rich reward if you can apply to me the same medicine which cured you!" And, saying this, he directed the gaze of Tranquillinus to an immense pile of pure gold, which gleamed and sparkled brightly in the dim candlelight. "If you can cure me," said he, "this shall all be yours!"

But Tranquillinus was unmoved by the sight of this treasure. He said, "Chromatius, it is on account of the wrath and fury of God that you are afflicted with this painful malady and nothing else. You are wrong to believe that the grace of God, which has the power to heal all our mortal pains and to overcome death itself, may either be brought or sold for earthly riches, by silver or by gold. All you must do is simply believe in Christ, the only-begotten Son of God, and then you will be liberated from your illness and restored to perfect well-being, even as I was.

"For I myself was held prisoner by the dreaded disease of gout. It tormented me so badly that I could barely move my limbs, and I needed to be carried around. Indeed, I could barely even carry a morsel of food to my own mouth without assistance. But the moment I believed in Christ, I was healed. His saving grace poured into every fiber of my being and renewed my youth and my strength. And now, as you can see, I stand upright and move about with perfect freedom and ease!"

The interest of Chromatius was greatly aroused by the testimony of Tranquillinus. He urged Tranquillinus to go forth at once and to hasten to bring to him the one who had initiated him into the Christian faith in order that he also could become a believer and thus be cured. So the old man went forth on nimble feet to the residence of Polycarp, the priest. And he related to him carefully all that had come to pass, telling him of the desire of Chromatius to accept the faith. Then both Tranquillinus and Polycarp went to the palace of Chromatius.

Upon seeing him, the prefect said to the priest, "Alas, I suffer from a painful and debilitating illness—the dreaded disease of gout. This prevents my moving around freely and makes my every waking moment a torment! Yet I know that you, with your particular doctrines and incantations, have the ability to liberate me from this condition. I pledge to you that I will give you whatever you ask—yes, even half of my wealth!—should you consent to cure me, just as you have evidently cured Tranquillinus."

Upon hearing this, Polycarp burst into laughter. "It is Christ Jesus," he said, "and no other, Who has the power to open for you the doors of grace and liberty. It is He alone who has the medicine which can restore you, body and soul, to perfect well-being. But offer me none of your wealth, and do not try to purchase my favor, nor that of God, with either silver or gold! For such earthly things have no real power and no real value. For human beings cannot purchase health for a sum of currency, nor life for a quantity of gold. On the contrary, those who seek to gain money and riches often inflict upon their own souls an incurable wound."

Chromatius was eager to learn what he must do to experience the healing power of which Polycarp spoke so eloquently. He implored him to reveal to him what was required of him. Polycarp told him that all he needed to do to receive the grace of God was to believe with all his heart, just as Tranquillinus had come to believe. The prefect inquired what was it which he was required to believe, for his notions of the Christian faith were but vague and confused at this point. And Polycarp promised to teach him with great joy.

And so it happened that the priest stayed at the residence of Chromatius and catechized him in the elements of the faith. He also summoned Sebastian to the palace of the prefect to assist him in the work of the instruction of Chromatius and to employ his own eloquence and wisdom to help him to understand the mysteries of the faith. And they all resolved to fast for three days in preparation for the administration of the holy sacrament of Baptism.

15

THUS IT WAS that Sebastian and Polycarp explained to Chromatius the infinite power of God, the wonders of the Holy Trinity, and the mystery of the incarnation of Christ. Moreover, they painted to him in vivid words the joys and glories of heaven and the endless tortures and torments of hell. "My friend," said Polycarp, "if you find it hard to bear the pains of your gout, however shall you endure the eternal torments of hell? If you struggle and suffer because of a condition which afflicts only your passing and corporeal body, however shall you carry the nameless agonies of the inferno, which suffuse the entire being, including the immortal soul, with unspeakable and unimaginable pain?"

After receiving the wise teaching of Polycarp and hearing the persuasive words of Sebastian, Chromatius was entirely convinced of the truth of the faith of which they spoke. But he did raise one concern which he had. "I believe what you say," he said, "but there is a matter which still worries me. I have noticed that many of the people who follow your creed are poor and ill-educated folk, servants and common laborers. If your faith contains such wisdom, why is it that it attracts these type of people in such multitudes?"

Sebastian replied, "It is often the way of God to enlighten the simple and to reveal His mysteries firstly to the humble. For the compassion of Christ went forth to the lowly and poor and those afflicted with suffering. And when God first created human beings, He made them as simple farmers and shepherds, not as orators or grammarians! Indeed, even in your own case, it was your infirmity which drew you to seek to learn our faith and not your power, wealth, or education."

Chromatius was then eager to be baptized, together with his young son Tibertius. He asked Polycarp if there was anything more he needed to do before this could take place. The holy priest was delighted to hear this. But as he looked around the luxurious palace of Chromatius, he noticed that it was adorned with a great many idols, some of glistening gold or shining silver, some of bright bronze and sparkling crystal, and some fashioned from skillfully carven wood and precious polished stone. "You must firstly destroy all of these ungodly abominations," he said gravely.

"For the person who wishes to draw clean water from a well must ensure that their bucket is first clean," he continued. "If he draws water into a bucket which is lined with filth and mud, the water which goes into the bucket will also become dirty. No, before drawing the clean water of your new faith, it behooves you firstly to cleanse your heart and house of all the filthy remnants of the pagan superstitions which you once served!"

Then Chromatius, filled with the fire of divine inspiration, turned upon the various idols which filled his house with fury and contempt. Some he shattered with a blow of his sword, whilst others he smashed on the ground, trampling underfoot their broken fragments. And as these images of false deities were destroyed, he felt a glorious liberty being infused into his heart as the chains of error and untruth fell from his soul.

Yet strangely, the pain of his gout remained.

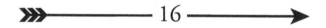

— 16 —

After Chromatius had destroyed all his idols, Polycarp and Sebastian both approached him and congratulated him. "Now that you believe," said Sebastian, "and have destroyed these false gods (or rather, demons) which you once worshiped and which held you in thrall, your soul must surely be delighted to taste the freedom of the children of God." The newly-converted prefect replied that he did indeed feel a hitherto unknown liberty and lightness within his heart.

Then Polycarp said to him, "And surely, also, you must be delighted to be freed from the physical torments of gout which had burdened you for so long?" But as he said these words, suddenly Chromatius became downcast, and a shadow of disappointment passed over his face. "Alas," said he, "the physical pain of which you speak has in no way abated. For even as I exerted my body in destroying the idols which had held me captive, my joints and limbs were racked with their customary discomfort. I fear that the healing which you promised me has not come!"

Upon hearing this, both Polycarp and Sebastian were perplexed. They inquired of the prefect if he had any other idols in his home or artifact or emblems of the pagan religion. Chromatius considered carefully, then, after a few moments of silence, he confessed, "I do possess an astrolabe, which I keep in a special upper chamber dedicated to its use. This is something I have inherited from my father, who was a most erudite scholar. He had this fine creation fashioned for himself, according to his own design and ingenuity, out of two hundred pounds of the purest gold. This astrolabe is a device for studying the movement of the stars, planets, and other celestial bodies. I have also a kind of mirror, made from transparent glass and fine crystal, in which the movement and changes in the star may be perceived with clarity, and the beams of light issuing from them may be analyzed. For the wisdom of the ancients has taught us that the waxing and waning of the moon, the trajectory of the stars in the vault of heaven, and the appearance of comets and meteors all have a relation to the events which transpire on earth, as expressed in the maxim of the illustrious philosophers, *As above, so below*."

With some hesitation, the prefect continued, "Yet surely this device, which encapsulates the learning of the sages of yore, is not to be considered a pagan artifact. Rather, it seems to be an innocent tool of scientific study."

Upon hearing about the astrolabe and the mirror, Polycarp was filled with horror and shook his head with consternation.

"Do you not know," he said grimly, "that the various planets, stars, and constellation which fill the night sky are known by the names of the demonic idols which conspire to corrupt and enslave the human race? For there is amongst them Jupiter and Saturn and Venus and Mars, and many others—indeed, the whole pantheon of false deities! In attributing such powers and intelligence to these celestial objects, you pay homage to the maleficent spirits whose names they bear. And do you not realize that it is none of these who actually control the events of history but rather solely the will of the one omnipotent God, Who made both the heavens and the earth and all that abides therein, and Who governs the entire cosmos by His wisdom and power?

"Nor can you have failed to observe that, although many people have earnestly applied their efforts and intelligence to determining accurate means of predicting the future, none have ever shown any real or consistent success. Indeed, demons tempt people with vain promises of being able to discern the future or to perform other deeds of magical art but are in reality utterly powerless to do anything of the kind. Take the case of astrological signs in foretelling a person's life. How many people are born under precisely the same star sign when precisely the same conditions prevail amongst the celestial bodies? Yet each of these people will have a different path of life. And each will come to a different end—some perishing from famine, some dying from disease, some being slaughtered in war, others drowning in shipwrecks, and yet others living to a good old age.

"Surely, if any person genuinely possessed the power to predict the future, they would soon attain to success and wealth beyond all calculation. But if one observes the practitioners of astrology, augury, necromancy, and other forms of divination, seldom are such people conspicuous for any particular worldly success! And what is more, they imperil their immortal souls for the sake of these deceptive diabolic promises, which offer no genuine rewards in return. How vain and foolish are all attempts to transcend the proper bounds of human knowledge, and how foolish it is to seek to attain blessing and assistance from any source except the one omnipotent God, Who alone possesses all power and rules this universe as its supreme King!

"You must destroy this astrolabe and this accursed mirror!" said Polycarp. "For it is only then that you shall find relief from the pains which afflict you; it is only thus that true and complete healing shall be yours."

And having been admonished in these terms by the sagacious man of God, Chromatius braced himself with firm resolve. He then took a hammer to the astrolabe and the magical mirror, destroying them utterly. And as their shattered pieces fell to the floor, the pain of his gout instantly ceased.

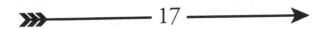

17

ONCE POLYCARP AND Sebastian saw the difficult sacrifice which Chromatius had made in destroying these wicked but precious objects, they rejoiced greatly. And Chromatius, perceiving himself to be freed from the pain of his gout for the first time in many years, was also overwhelmed with happiness and new hope. He entreated Polycarp to baptize both him and his son Tibertius without further delay.

But at this point, Sebastian stepped forward to offer him some wise counsel. "Chromatius," he said, "you know that I am employed as a soldier of the Roman army and serve as the commander of the first imperial cohort. I keep my faith concealed and endeavor to go about the business of my profession with commitment and competence. The reason I do this is so that I am in a position to encourage and assist others who are facing persecution at the hands of the imperial authorities. It was in this way that I have been able to strengthen and confirm Marcus and Marcellianus, the two sons of Tranquillinus, and also bring about the conversion of a great many others. But I am merely a soldier, and it is relatively easy for me not to draw attention to myself or my faith.

"But for you, it is a completely different matter. As prefect of Rome, you are a prominent person and the object of much public attention. You wield great power and influence and are called to make decisions affecting the whole city and to preside at official ceremonies. It will not be possible for you to keep your faith as a private matter, nor will it be possible for you to fulfil your public office without acting contrary to that faith to which you shall soon pledge yourself in baptism. Therefore I advise you to feign illness and ask to be relieved of your duties as prefect. Then you must leave behind this palace and all your riches and forget completely your past life and status. Then you may commence your life as a Christian as someone newly born—for indeed the sacrament of Baptism is truly a second birth through which one comes forth as a child of God!"

Chromatius realized the wisdom and necessity of what Sebastian recommended. He agreed to do as he said. And then the formal ceremony of his enrollment for baptism began. Polycarp first asked him if he believed in the Christian faith and accepted the creed and doctrines of the Church. To this Chromatius replied, "I do so believe." Then he asked him if he renounced all his idols. To which he similarly indicated that he did. Finally, the priest asked him if he renounced all his former sins. To this, the prefect said, "It is fitting that you ask me this question! Yes, I renounce all my sins, lest any stain remain on me after my baptism. All the foolish wrath with which I once blazed so fiercely, I renounce. All the debts which are owed to me by others, I remit. Everything which I have seized by violence and exhortation, I return to its rightful owners.

"Since my wife passed away, I confess that I have maintained two concubines to satisfy the carnal lusts of my flesh. These I shall immediately dismiss from my household. As for all my slaves and indentured servants, I grant to them all unconditional freedom."

Upon hearing these sincere words of repentance, the son of Chromatius, Tibertius, then spoke up. "My father," said the wise youth, "do not hesitate also to renounce all your wealth and property for the sake of the kingdom of heaven. I know that you are reluctant to do this, not for your own sake, but for my sake, since it is I who stand to inherit it. Nevertheless, like you, I would gladly choose poverty in this passing world for the sake of the eternal treasures of heaven; happily will I spend my earthly days in humility and lowliness in order to attain to the glory which has no end!"

Thus encouraged by the words of his son, Chromatius (who was immensely rich) added to his series of renunciations a resolution to give away all that he possessed in the present world.

Shortly afterwards, when Chromatius had put into effect all that he had promised, both he and Tibertius were baptized. And Saint Sebastian himself acted as godfather to Tibertius. And not only these two but also all the slaves and servant to whom Chromatius had granted liberty received the sacrament of Christian Baptism. And he declared to them, "Since you have all become sons or daughters of God, never again shall you bow your heads to any human master!" The former slaves and servants whom Chromatius released, who had worked on his many farms and estates throughout Italy, numbered some 6,400.

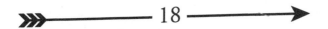

18

IN THOSE DAYS, Pope Caius governed the Church as pontiff of Rome.[21] He was a man of great prudence and impeccable virtue, and he served as pope during the reign of the emperors Carinus, Diocletian, and Maximian. At that time, only Diocletian and Maximian were present in Rome, for Carinus was in France leading the army there. It was whilst Carinus was absent that Diocletian and Maximian commenced their rabid and cruel campaign of persecutions of Christians.[22] Carinus, on the other hand, considered Christians to be his friends and often spoke highly of their virtue, courage, and moral rectitude.

The persecution of Christianity had reached such a height of tyranny that people were forbidden from either buying or sell-

---

[21] Pope Saint Caius governed the Church from 283 to 296. He is believed to have suffered martyrdom under Diocletian.

[22] Carinus was the elder son of the emperor Carus Caesar, but Diocletian (who had been a military leader) usurped the imperial crown from him. Very little is known with certainty about Carinus; it is possible that he was a Christian.

ing anything unless they first paid verbal homage to the gods of Rome and declared their allegiance to them. And official guards were appointed to enforce these draconian restrictions with the utmost vigilance and severity. In this way, Christians were effectively excluded from partaking in the normal business of life, and a wave of fear and suspicion prevailed everywhere.

In response to this dire situation, Pope Caius suggested to Chromatius that he, together with any Christians who wanted to join him, should relocate themselves to a large estate which he owned in the province of Campania.[23] In this way, said he, they would be able to live relatively comfortably and safely, until the cruel persecutions had come to any end. To this proposal, Chromatius gladly agreed.

News of this development quickly spread through the community of Christians in Rome. And many resolved to leave Rome until conditions for them there had improved. Nevertheless, a contention arose between Polycarp and Sebastian. For both were eager to remain in Rome in order to have the honor of risking martyrdom for the sake of their faith. But Caius intervened, declaring that Polycarp should proceed to Campania with Chromatius and the other Christians in order to attend to their pastoral needs. As for Sebastian, with his intelligence, strength, and energy, Caius said that he should stay in Rome to assist and protect the remaining Christians in whatever way he could.

---

[23] In southern Italy.

But Tibertius, the young son of Chromatius, strongly objected to taking refuge in Campania. Inflamed with enthusiasm for his new faith, he said he would not flee from persecution but remain in Rome and assist Sebastian. He implored Pope Caius, "O holy Father and prelate of prelates, I beg you, permit me to stay here in this city. For to me it will be an honor and happiness to face peril and danger for the sake of my faith so that I may prove myself to be a true and courageous solider of the Lord! For I know that by fighting for God, and by dying for Him, I shall attain a glorious reward which will endure forever and which none may ever steal from my grasp!"

Upon hearing these words, the holy pontiff was filled with admiration of the lad's zeal and bravery. Pouring out tears of emotion, he prayed that all the Christians who remained in Rome to confront the persecution head on should emerge as victors in the battle and come to attain the glorious golden crown of sacred martyrdom.

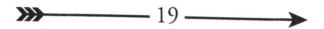 19

THUS IT HAPPENED that Pope Caius, together with Sebastian and
Tibertius, remained in Rome during the height of the persecution. Also present through this time were the two brothers Marcus and Marcellianus; Tranquillinus, their father; Nicostratus,
the imperial magistrate, together with his brother, Castor, and his
wife, Zoe. Also Claudius, the officer of Nicostratus, remained,
together with his brother Victorinus and his son Felicissimus[24]
(who had been cured from fluid retention). They stayed in the
capital city, whilst all other members of the Christian community went forth with Chromatius to the safety of Campania.

Pope Caius wished to honor this group who had chosen to
remain and exhibited such courage in facing martyrdom without fear. So he ordained both Marcus and Marcellianus as dea-

---

[24] Here, the Latin text gives the name Symphronius, but the son in question was iden-
tified by the name of Felicissimus earlier. This may be a narrative error, or he may have
been known by two names (one Latin and one Greek). Felicissimus has been given in the
translation for the sake of clarity.

cons. Their elderly father, Tranquillinus, he ordained as a priest. To Saint Sebastian, who had rendered such powerful support to so many Christians, he gave the honorific title of "Defender of the Church." And all the other men, [Nicostratus, Castor, Claudius, Victorinus, and Felicissimus], he ordained as sub-deacons.

Now there was a certain supervisor of a palace called Castulus who was a secret Christian. Since the palace was otherwise uninhabited at that time and Castulus was acting as a kind of caretaker, he was able to offer it for use to the pope, Sebastian, and the other members of their group. And it proved to be an ideal hiding place for them, with adequate space for prayer, sleeping, and the other necessities of life.

This deserted palace, in due course, came to be a center for the faithful who remained in Rome, although it was kept as a strict secret within the circle of believers. Many would come to Caius or Sebastian to implore their prayers. A great multitude of persons experienced miraculous healings, sight was restored to the blind, hearing was imparted to the deaf, the lame were made to walk, and lepers were cleansed. Thus it came to pass that in that time of the most dire persecution, the flame of faith continued to burn strongly in the hearts of believers, and, indeed, many new converts came to embrace the faith.

One particular incident is worthy of inclusion in this present narrative. It happened that Tibertius was out walking in the streets of Rome one day when he passed by a certain tall building site. Now a young man who had been working at the site fell from an immense height and plummeted to the hard pavement of the street below. His skull was shattered, and his whole body was horribly broken. Many people, including the parents of the young man, stood by aghast at the grotesque sight, weeping and wailing in shock and sorrow.

But Tibertius approached the scene of horror confidently and said, "Permit me to pray for him. Who knows? Perhaps he will recover." And having spoken thus, he made the sign of the cross over the mutilated body and quietly recited the Lord's Prayer and the Creed. And—behold!—the shattered bones and smashed flesh reassembled itself to full soundness. The young man then rose to his feet alive and well, as if nothing at all had happened to him!

At this point, Tibertius was about to walk away. But the parents of the young man whom he had miraculously restored to life clasped him and said, "Take our son as your servant, we implore you! For he was dead and you have restored him to life, and so his life rightfully belongs to you. Indeed, take us both into your service as well, and let us serve you faithfully all the days of our lives. For your marvelous power makes it fitting that we should honor you as our lord and master!"

But Tibertius refused their offer. Instead, he explained that what had happened was due to no power or merits of his own but of the one true God and His only-begotten Son, Jesus Christ. When the details of the Christian faith had been explained to them by Tibertius, they were eager to be baptized as soon as possible. So Tibertius, seeing them filled with genuine fear of God, brought them with him back to the hiding place of Pope Caius in the abandoned palace. There, the pontiff baptized them, giving thanks to God for the miracle he had worked through Tibertius that day.

20

IF WE WISHED to describe in detail the martyrdom of all those who embraced the faith in those times thanks to the words and example of Saint Sebastian and to tell of all the remarkable wonders which Christ worked through this brave company of saints, we should need to extend our work to almost limitless length. So we shall instead narrate how just one of these—Zoe, the wife of Nicostratus—came to receive the splendid crown of martyrdom from God. This Zoe is the same woman who had lost her voice for some six years and had been cured through the prayers of Saint Sebastian. Truly, she demonstrated wonderfully the virtue, fidelity, and courage which was equally possessed by all the others.

On the feast day of the apostles Saint Peter and Saint Paul, blessed Zoe was praying at a church dedicated to Saint Peter when suddenly a band of pagans surrounded her and arrested her. They led her to the local magistrate. This particular magistrate was an avid supporter of, and participant in, the campaign of cruel persecution of all Christians instigated by Diocletian and Maximian.

As Zoe stood before the magistrate, he indicated to her a small, marble statue of the god Mars which stood in his court, and he demanded that she should burn incense before it. But she answered him disdainfully, saying, "Will you force me, a woman, to sacrifice to Mars? Is it that you want to prove that this false god of yours is a favorite with the fair sex? Well, maybe he was able to count Venus amongst his conquests! But he shall never win *my* favors or prevail against my virtue, since I carry within my heart the treasure of faith. Yet I do not claim to fight against him with my own strength. No, I place all my confidence and trust in the power of my Lord Jesus Christ. I laugh at both you and Mars, your feeble and absurd idol!"

The wicked magistrate was enraged and indignant, and he ordered that Zoe be confined in one of his darkest and smallest dungeons. There, she was held entirely without any light for a period of five days. Neither did she receive anything to eat or drink. But the cruel magistrate spoke to her from outside her unlit cell, and these were his ominous and menacing words: "You shall die of starvation and thirst in the squalor of utter darkness, my lady, unless you consent to honor the gods of Rome!"

After Zoe had been confined in this way for some five days, however, the magistrate realized that she was not going to give in to his demand. So, on the sixth day, he ordered that she be taken out of the dungeon and suspended from a tree by a rope tied around her neck and her hair. Moreover, he ordered that a blazing fire be lit beneath her, fueled by dung so that it gave off clouds of dense and noxious smoke. This was carried out, and the brave woman gave forth her spirit to the Lord whilst proclaiming her faith in Jesus Christ. The guards and executioners then tied her body to a large rock and hurled it into the murky depths of the River Tiber, lest other Christians should retrieve her holy remains and come to venerate her as a saint.[25]

Once Zoe had undergone her heroic martyrdom, she appeared shortly afterward to Sebastian in a dream. And she narrated to him how she had faced death for the sake of her fidelity to the Lord. A little time later, Sebastian related to Tranquillinus what he had heard in this dream. Upon hearing this, Tranquillinus was filled with awe and admiration, and he threw himself to the ground, saying, "This noble and faithful woman has achieved the crown of holy martyrdom already! And yet here am I, an old man, and still I continue to live."

But a little later, on the eighth day after the feast of Saint Peter and Saint Paul, Tranquillinus himself became a martyr. For, while he was deep in prayer at a church dedicated to the apostle Saint Paul, a crowd of vicious pagans seized him and stoned him to death. Then they hurled his lifeless and battered corpse into the River Tiber to sink beneath its hungry waves.

A few days after this, Nicostratus and Claudius—together with Castor, Victorianus, and Felicissimus—went searching on the banks of the mighty Tiber in the hope of finding the bodies

---

[25] In the Latin, "*faciant sibi illam deam*" ("make her into a goddess for themselves"). This expression seems to reflect the guards' misunderstanding concerning the Christian veneration of saints.

of Zoe and Tranquillinus washed up from their watery graves. Yet, as they were doing this, they were detected and captured by the imperial persecutors of the Church. These led them before the new prefect of Rome, Fabian. [This Fabian had become prefect following the conversion of the previous prefect, Chromatius, to Christianity, as detailed in this narrative.]

Fabian urged them to offer sacrifice before the traditional gods of the empire, and he promised them that for ten days, they would suffer no punishment. Indeed, it was his intention during this time to coerce them by the bloodless means of bribes and threats to renounce their faith.

But the emperors Diocletian and Maximian heard about the prisoners and sent orders that from the third day onwards, they were to be subjected to physical tortures. But it soon became clear that even under the compulsion of physical pain, these brave men were not going to be shaken from their loyalty to Christ. And so the prefect commanded that they be chained to heavy rocks, taken out by a ship into the sea, and then thrown into the fathomless depths. Thus it was that in the dark waters of the ocean, they attained the radiant crown of martyrdom.

In such a manner did the faithless pagans lay snares for the faithful Christians in those dreadful days. For, indeed, the pagans were so vexed by a godless and demonic fury that they could scarcely bear even to hear the name of "Christian" without resorting to rabid and bloodthirsty violence.

21

A LITTLE WHILE after this, a certain young man by the name of Torquatus joined himself with the small band of Christians headed by Pope Caius and Sebastian. He asserted that he was a faithful follower of Christ, but he was, in fact, an imposter and fraud. He tried to corrupt the group by sowing doubts amongst them and raising questions about the value of fasting, keeping vigil, and spending long hours in prayer. He particularly tried to attach himself to Tibertius and to tempt him to stray from his holy manner of life. Torquatus, unlike Tibertius, was gluttonous and insatiable in his feasting, and he loved the debauchery of copious winebibbing. And although he tried to be patient and tolerant, Tibertius was offended by Torquatus and disliked his disdain for true piety and devotion.

Now it came about that both youths were arrested together by the imperial authorities and taken before the prefect Fabian. Fabian began by questioning Torquatus. "Are you a Christian?"

he enquired. To this, he answered, "Yes, I am. And my companion is the one who has converted me to the Christian faith. For he is a leader of that sect." Upon hearing this, Fabian turned his attention to Tiberius, "Is this true? Are you a leader of the Christians and a promoter of that creed?"

Tiberius replied, "Nothing that Torquatus has said is true. For, though I am a Christian, I am certainly not a leader nor a teacher. Moreover, Torquatus also lies when he says he is a Christian. For his morals and manner of life show that he has nothing in common with us!"

Fabian was greatly surprised at this and perplexed about how to proceed in the situation. Nevertheless, he was impressed by the courage, honesty, and humility of Tiberius. He warned the youth, "Surely you are aware of the decree of our noble emperor imposing torture and death upon all those who profess themselves to be Christians. At this time, you would be well advised to give better consideration to your own well-being!"

To this, Tiberius retorted, "I can give no better consideration to my own well-being, both of body and soul, than by adhering with absolute loyalty to the one true God, the Lord Jesus Christ, and treating with contempt all your false idols of wood and stone and metal. For in Christ alone is our salvation to be found!"

At this point, the imposter Torquatus interjected, "As you can see, Your Excellency, Tiberius is a fervent and fanatical Christian. Not only does he proclaim Christ to be the only true God, but he declares the gods of Rome to be falsehoods and vanities."

But Tibertius interjected, "This weak-souled wretch, Torquatus, though he declared himself to be a Christian, is not to be numbered amongst us. For if you ever saw him eating, you would see that he is as greedy as a Cyclops. And he loves nothing more than to drown himself in wine! This is not what a Christian does. Therefore, let this pathetic coward go free.

"As for those of us who are *true* Christians, I say, send forth your torturers and your executioners to us! Punish us, torment us, do whatever you will. For we shall not fall away or waver. If you send us into exile, we will reply (like the true philosophers we are) that this whole mortal life is really nothing but an exile. If you sentence us to death, we shall reply that through earthly death you release us from the prison of this valley of tears and send us forth to the glories of paradise. If you sentence us to flames, we shall say that we have conquered more acrid fires than these in learning to tame the lusts of the flesh. Do whatsoever you please! For the person whose conscience is pure fears absolutely nothing."

Upon hearing this, Fabian was enflamed with wrath and diabolical fury. He ordered a tray of red-hot burning coals to be placed before Tibertius. And he said to him, "I give you a choice, Tibertius. Either sprinkle a little incense upon these coals in honor of the gods of Rome or, if you refuse to do that, you shall walk over them with bare feet!"

Tibertius did not hesitate, but blessed himself with the sign of the cross. Removing his sandals, he walked across the hot coals as if he were walking upon a pleasant lawn. And he said to all those present, "Leave behind your blind superstitions and learn to worship the one true God, Who governs the whole universe by His wisdom and power. If any of you dare, then come and join me on these hot coals, invoking the name of Jupiter or Jove, or whomsoever you please! And if Jupiter or any other false deity is able to help you, then surely they will. But as for me, the holy name of the Lord Jesus Christ protects me, and I stand upon these glowing coals like a person standing upon a bed of delightful flowers. For all of creation serves our God and obeys His behests."

But Fabian was furious. He retorted, "Who is there who does not realize that this Christ of yours is a nothing more than an exponent of magical arts? You have blasphemed the ancient gods, and the blade of the sword shall confirm your guilt!"

And so it was that Tiburtius was forcibly taken along the Via Lavacano about three miles from the city of Rome. And there, while he poured forth prayers to heaven, he was beheaded with a single stroke of the sword.

Some Christians who lived in the area found his body a little later and buried the young martyr with due reverence and honor.

22

AFTER THE EXECUTION of Tiburtius, the cowardly imposter Torquatus revealed to the Roman officials the secret hiding place of Pope Caius, Sebastian, and the other Christians in the deserted palace of Castulus. These were all arrested and brought before Fabian, the prefect.

Firstly, Castulus himself met his death, and attained the golden crown of martyrdom. A deep pit was dug, and he was hurled into it. After these, copious loads of sand were emptied upon him until he was crushed to death. And thus, while his mortal body was submerged in the earth, his immortal soul migrated to the ineffable glories of heaven.

Next, Marcus and Marcellianus were cruelly killed. Fabian had them both bound and nailed by their feet to wooden crosses. And he said to them, "As long as you refuse to give due honor to the ancient gods of Rome, you shall remain affixed to this wood!" But the brethren both remained steadfast. Indeed, they continued to chant without cessation that verse of the psalm, "How good and pleasant it is for brothers to dwell in unity!"[26]

In this manner, Marcus and Marcellianus continued for an entire day and entire night. Despite the agony they experienced, never did they pause from their joyful chanting as they looked forward to the joys of heaven.

Finally, Fabian lost his patience and ordered them to be driven through with spears. And thus they expired, gaining for themselves the unfading glory of holy martyrdom and entering into the star-illuminated kingdom of eternal peace and bliss.

And the bodies of these two noble saints were buried in the Via Appia, two miles from the city of Rome.

---

[26] Psalm 132:1.

 23

AFTER ALL OF these things had taken place, Sebastian himself was arrested by the imperial spies. Since he was a man of high rank in the Roman army and court, he was taken before the emperor Diocletian for a personal audience.

Diocletian looked upon Sebastian with some sadness and disappointment. At last, he exclaimed, "Sebastian, I have always held you to be one of my most trustworthy and capable officers, and I have given you a distinguished place in my court. And yet you, in return, have betrayed both the ancient gods of Rome and myself! You have been an enemy to me, a spy and traitor, hiding yourself beneath the military garments of a soldier of the empire."

Sebastian raised his eyes to him and replied with all sincerity, "My Emperor, I have worshiped Christ, it is true. But I have done this always for the sake of your own well-being and preservation. Yes, I have adored the one God of heaven for the benefit

of the great empire of Rome, as well as for the salvation of my
own soul! For I have come to realize how foolish and vain it is to
seek assistance from false idols, from gods made of lifeless stone,
when it is only the true God who can help and protect us."

But Diocletian, despite the gentleness and honesty of Sebastian's words, was filled with black fury. He commanded that
his former friend and officer should be taken out to a field and
bound to a pole. There, he was to be shot at with arrows until
he expired. So the soldiers led him forth and did just as was
commanded. They shot so many arrows into him that his body
came to resemble that of a hedgehog, with innumerable spikes
protruding from every part of it.

So, supposing him to be dead, they left him where he was,
tied to the pole, perforated with countless wounds and bleed-
ing profusely. That night, the widow of the Castulus, the palace
caretaker—who had been martyred earlier—a woman by the
name of Irene, came to recover the corpse of Sebastian so that
she might give him an honorable Christian burial. But, to her
utter amazement, she discovered that he was still living! She took
him to her house, and within a few days, he had entirely recov-
ered from his many wounds, with his health and limbs restored
to perfect soundness and vigor.

When the local Christians heard about this miracle, they all
came to see Sebastian. And they urged him to go into hiding to
escape the wrath of Diocletian. But he, on the contrary, prayed
to God and then proceeded straight to the imperial palace. There
he stood boldly on the steps. And when the two co-emperors,
Diocletian and Maximian, passed by, he reproached them vehe-

mently and vociferously. "Your Majesties, the high priests of the pagan gods are laying wicked snares to souls and to the whole empire of Rome. For they make false accusations against Christians, labelling them as enemies of the state. But this is simply not true! For we who believe in the one true God never cease to pray to Him for the good of the people of Rome and the peace and prosperity of the empire."

Diocletian was bewildered and perplexed to see Sebastian still alive and healthy. He said in astonishment, "Are you really the same Sebastian whom I ordered to be shot with arrows, and whom my soldiers informed me was dead?" To this the saint replied, "Indeed I am! For the Lord Jesus Christ has deigned to restore me to the fullness of life and health, as you can plainly see. And He did this so that I could give testimony to Him in the presence of all the people and declare the injustice of your cruel persecution of Christians and of the holy Church."

Diocletian was infuriated, and ordered Sebastian to be taken to the stadium and there to be clubbed to death. This was promptly done, and the saint gave forth his noble and courageous spirit to God, his faithful soul ascending to the infinite glories of heaven.

The soldiers took his body that night and threw it scornfully into the great sewer of Rome, saying, "This way the Christians will not be able to find his remains and venerate him as a martyr."

But a little while later, the spirit of Saint Sebastian appeared in a dream to a certain religious woman called Lucila. He said to her, "My daughter, I am the ghost of Sebastian, who was recently put to death for my refusal to renounce to Christ, my true Lord. My earthly body now lies in the great sewer. Please go forth and recover it, then bury me in the catacombs at the feet of the bodies of the holy apostles!"

So Lucila called some of her trusted servants to her, and immediately they went forth and found Sebastian's body lying in the great sewer, just as he had told her in her dream. And they carefully placed him in a small wagon and transported his remains to the catacombs. There he was buried with all reverence and piety. As for Lucila herself, she remained present at his tomb in prayer and holy contemplation for some thirty days.

After the persecution of the Christians under Diocletian and Maximian had come to its end and the Church once more enjoyed the blessing of peace, she converted her house into a convent and used her considerable wealth to give daily alms to the poor. And after her death, Lucila bequeathed all her money and property to the support of Christians—to the glory of the eternal and omnipotent King of the Universe, our Lord Jesus Christ, Who, together with the Father and the Holy Spirit, lives and reigns forever and ever. Amen.

Here ends the Acts of Saint Sebastian and his companions.

Prayer to Saint Sebastian

Saint Sebastian, holy martyr,
Who gave your very blood for God,
Impart to us your dauntless courage,
To walk the noble path you trod.

Teach us to disdain all peril,
With courage to resist all fear,
That we may proclaim Christ's Gospel,
Heralds proud and strong and clear!

When the arrows of misfortune
Or the foe's malicious darts
Strike us with demonic hatred,
Pierce our skin and wound our hearts—

Then bestow your kind protection,
Fortify us with your might,
That we may be true and constant,
Ever-ready for the fight.

Make us share with you the triumph
Due to faith and holy love,
Keep our minds fixed on the glory
Promised to God's saints above.

Pray for us, O Saint Sebastian,
Intercede before God's throne,
Gain for us Christ's kind assistance
Through the merits you have shown.

To the Father be all glory,
And to His eternal Son,
United by the Holy Spirit,
Trinity forever One.

Amen.